BIG WHITE PUFFY THING

TANIA HOFF
ILLUSTRATED BY RUSTY

Ordering Information:

Prime Seven Media
518 Landmann St.
Tomah City, WI 54660

Printed in the United States of America

DEDICATION

To my husband **Stan** and my children **Sky** and **Teka** –
You inspire me in all you do. Thank you for the support
all these years. My awesome cheerleaders!

To: Rusty, Thank you for your artwork and reaching
your inner child. It means everything to me.

EARLY IN THE MORNING WHEN noOne WAS AROUND

1

the wind blew A BIG WHITE PUFFY THING

UP OFF
THE

GROUND

AT FIRST
I LAUGHED
HA HA AND THOUGHT
NOTHING OF IT.
UNTIL....

ALMOST 2

FEET OFF THE

GROUND

(AND CHANGED IT'S

SHAPE WITH

EVERY JUMP!)

BUT THERE ✓ WERE

NO EYES 👀
EARS 👂👂
NOSE 👃
OR
MOUTH 👄

IT WAS ONLY WHITE PUFFY AND...

WIND BLEW

IT

UP OFF

THE

GROUND

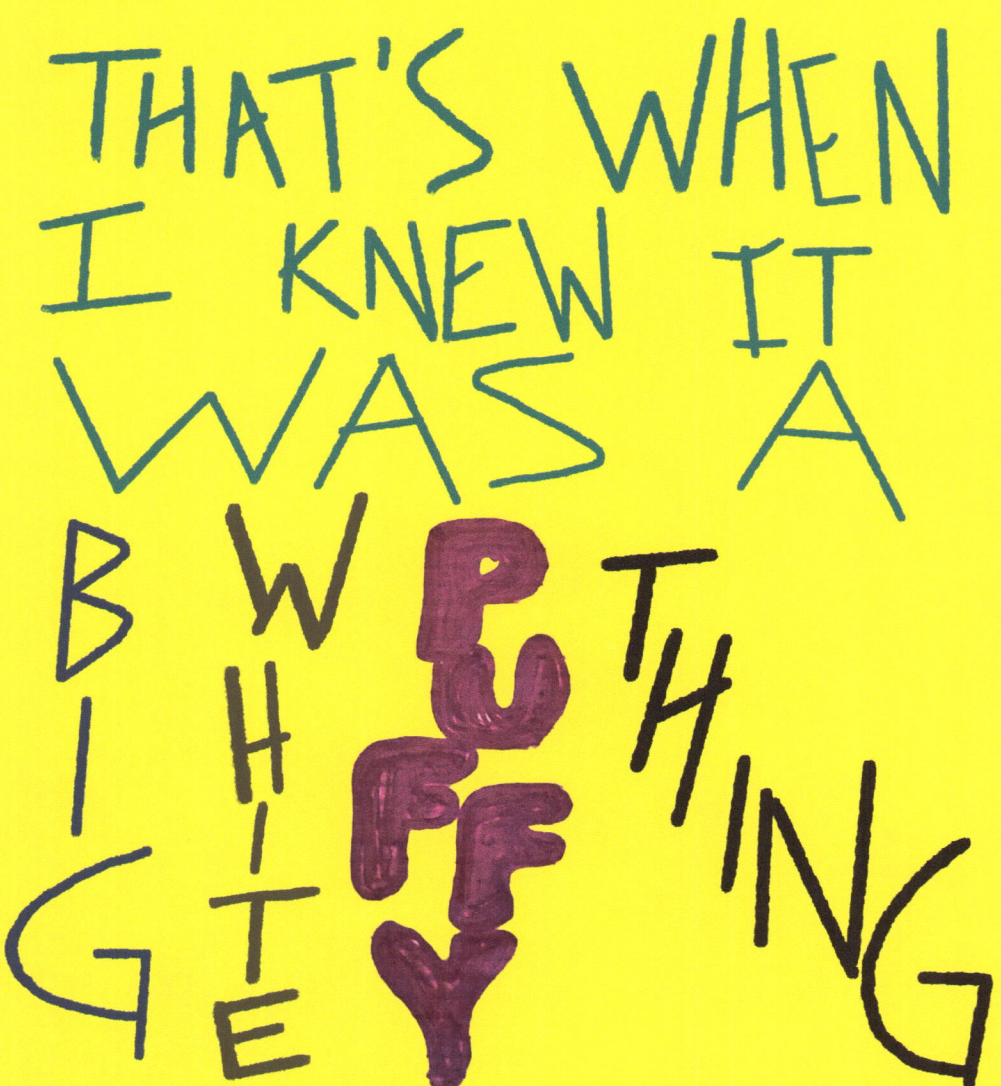

THAT'S WHEN I KNEW IT WAS A BIG WHITE PUFFY THING

YOU CARRY GROCERIES IN

14

NOT AN ALIEN!

www.ingramcontent.com/pod-product-compliance
Lightning Source LLC
Chambersburg PA
CBHW041614120626

46551CB00002B/438